This is an orchestra.

An orchestra sits in a fan.

woodwind **drums**

The louder instruments are at the back.

horns

strings

The wind instruments

bassoon

clarinet

French horn

trumpet

The stringed instruments

The drums

The conductor

baton

The conductor keeps the orchestra together.

An orchestra can have
a hundred or more
instruments.